World War II Parade Uniforms of the Soviet Union - Volume II

Marshal Stalin, President Roosevelt, and Prime Minister Churchill at the Russian Embassy in Teheran, November 28 to December 1, 1943

World War II Parade Uniforms of the Soviet Union - Volume II

Marshals, Generals, and Admirals

The Sinclair Collection

by James C. McComb Sinclair II
& Douglas A. Drabik

Schiffer Military History
Atglen, PA

Acknowledgments

Thanks again to my friend and colleague Doug Drabik for research, writing, and his help assembling this book. I would also like to thank my wife Ann and daughter Elizabeth for their love and help. Thanks again to Cheryl Lamoreux for her assistance in editing the text. Thanks also to Bob Biondi for direction and insight.

This book is the result of many other people's efforts: Vaughn Obern, Ilia Shapiro, Ted Drabik, Gary Van Loon, Nancy Drabik, Robert Yoder III, Bill Dienna, Tod Rathbone, and Shawn Caza.

Dedication

I dedicate this book to my wife Ann and daughter Elizabeth, who are always by my side in love, joy, and hope.

Library of Congress Control Number: 2004117385

Printed in China.
ISBN: 978-0-7643-4579-1

We are interested in hearing from authors with book ideas on related topics.

Published by Schiffer Publishing Ltd.
4880 Lower Valley Road
Atglen, PA 19310
Phone: (610) 593-1777
FAX: (610) 593-2002
E-mail: Info@schifferbooks.com.
Visit our web site at: **www.schifferbooks.com**
Please write for a free catalog.
This book may be purchased from the publisher.
Try your bookstore first.

Foreword

The 2005 publication of the first volume of *World War II Parade Uniforms of the Soviet Union* opened up for exploration a visual and scholarly study of a new frontier in military collecting. That stunning book allowed readers to examine uniforms previously only on display in the former USSR museums, or in only a few very advanced private collections.

The knowledge and understanding of the history of the Soviet military is relatively new and is constantly evolving. While the collecting of militaria of the former Soviet armed forces has grown in the last twenty years, the availability of the higher end and rarest of these items has all but disappeared. Fostering its reputation as the finest compendium of this type, the Sinclair Collection has added to its premier collection of Soviet general officers' parade uniforms. The authors' goal in these two volumes is to give the collector and historian access to original uniforms and photographs of the era that were not available for the first volume. The uniforms of the Sinclair Collection presented here, as in the first volume, represent some of the most rare, ornate, and striking uniforms of the high command of the Soviet armed forces during World War II.

The authors hope the readers enjoy these new additions to one of the most comprehensive Soviet uniform collections.

Douglas A. Drabik

General of the Army Zhukov in his M1940 uniform.

Contents

Foreword 5

Introduction 9

Chapter One M1940 Parade Uniform 13

Chapter Two M1943 Parade Uniforms 21

Chapter Three M1943 Service, Dress White Uniforms and Overcoats 55

Chapter Four M1945 Victory Parade Uniforms 81

Bibliography 160

His Excellency Yuri V. Ushakov, Ambassador Extraordinary and Plenipotentiary, and James C. McComb Sinclair II at the Embassy of the Russian Federation.

Introduction

With great pleasure I present *World War II Parade Uniforms of the Soviet Union, Volume II*. I thought that the first book was going to be a one-volume edition. The appearance of high end Soviet uniforms had all but disappeared from the market. The few examples that did come up for sale seldom made it to the United States. Since Volume I went to press, I have been very fortunate to find additional uniforms. This new volume features several very rare uniforms, including one of Generalissimus Stalin's, several branch Marshals, and many other rare examples. This book is a wonderful "go to source" for the World War II Soviet uniform collector. I doubt that a uniform collection such as this could ever be put together again, and I am gratified in knowing that this compendium has been kept intact and preserved. I would like to thank His Excellency Yuri V. Ushakov, Ambassador Extraordinary & Plenipotentiary for inviting me to exhibit part of the collection at the Embassy of the Russian Federation in Washington, D.C., and for accepting a copy of Volume I. I can't tell you how wonderful it was to speak with the many Soviet World War II veterans who were there to accept their 60th Anniversary medals. The veterans' heartfelt appreciation and understanding of the collection humbled me, and I was very touched by their kind words. These are memories that I will always cherish.

James C. McComb Sinclair II

General Timoshenko delivering a speech prior to being promoted to marshal.

Marshals of the Soviet Union Voroshilov, Budenny, Timoshenko, Kulik, and Shaposhnikov in M1940 parade uniforms.

Photograph of Marshal of the Soviet Union Timoshenko.

CHAPTER ONE

M1940 PARADE UNIFORM

While the M1935 uniform regulations instituted the rank of Marshal of the USSR, the corresponding uniform of that time did not seem to reflect the power and importance of the rank. A true reflection of the highest of Red Army ranks had to wait five more years for the introduction of the M1940 series of uniforms.

As described in Volume I of *World War II Parade Uniforms of the Soviet Union*, the M1940 Marshal of the USSR uniform followed the practice of all Red Army officers of that rank in tunic collar and cuff decoration. The most ornate rank insignia drawn up in 1940 was for Marshals of the USSR.

M1940 PARADE DRESS UNIFORM

FOR MARSHAL OF THE SOVIET UNION
SEMEN KONSTANTINOVICH TIMOSHENKO

While the M1940 uniform of Marshal of the USSR Semen Timoshenko, shown in Volume I, was made of a heavy, olive-green, almost overcoat-like material, the uniform shown opposite is of the standard grey material used on generals' and Marshals' M1940 parade uniforms. Other than the material, an added gold piping on the collar and a slight difference in medal and order placement, the uniforms are identical in design.

Marshal of the USSR Timoshenko was one of a handful of Ukrainians to rise to the highest rank in the Red Army under the rule of Stalin. Early on, Timoshenko was one of the former members of the Tsarist army who was able to make the transition to the Red Army.

Timoshenko's career was first set on its path after meeting and befriending Stalin during the Russian Civil War, and later serving under Marshal of the USSR Budenny in the First Cavalry Army. Remaining steadfastly loyal to Stalin, Timoshenko survived the purges that gutted the high command of the Red Army and led to his rapid rise to a high command position.

Timoshenko's breaking of the Mannerheim Line in the Winter War with Finland earned him promotion to Marshal of the USSR and the title of People's Commissar of Defense.

During the Great Patriotic War, Timoshenko was overshadowed by the rise of Marshal of the USSR Georgi Zhukov, and after 1942 he assumed mostly overseer roles in the Red Army.

Marshal Timoshenko was awarded The Order of Victory, five Orders of Lenin, five Orders of the Red Banner, three Orders of Suvorov, and numerous foreign awards.

Marshal Timoshenko died on March 2, 1970, and was laid to rest in Red Square at the Kremlin Wall.

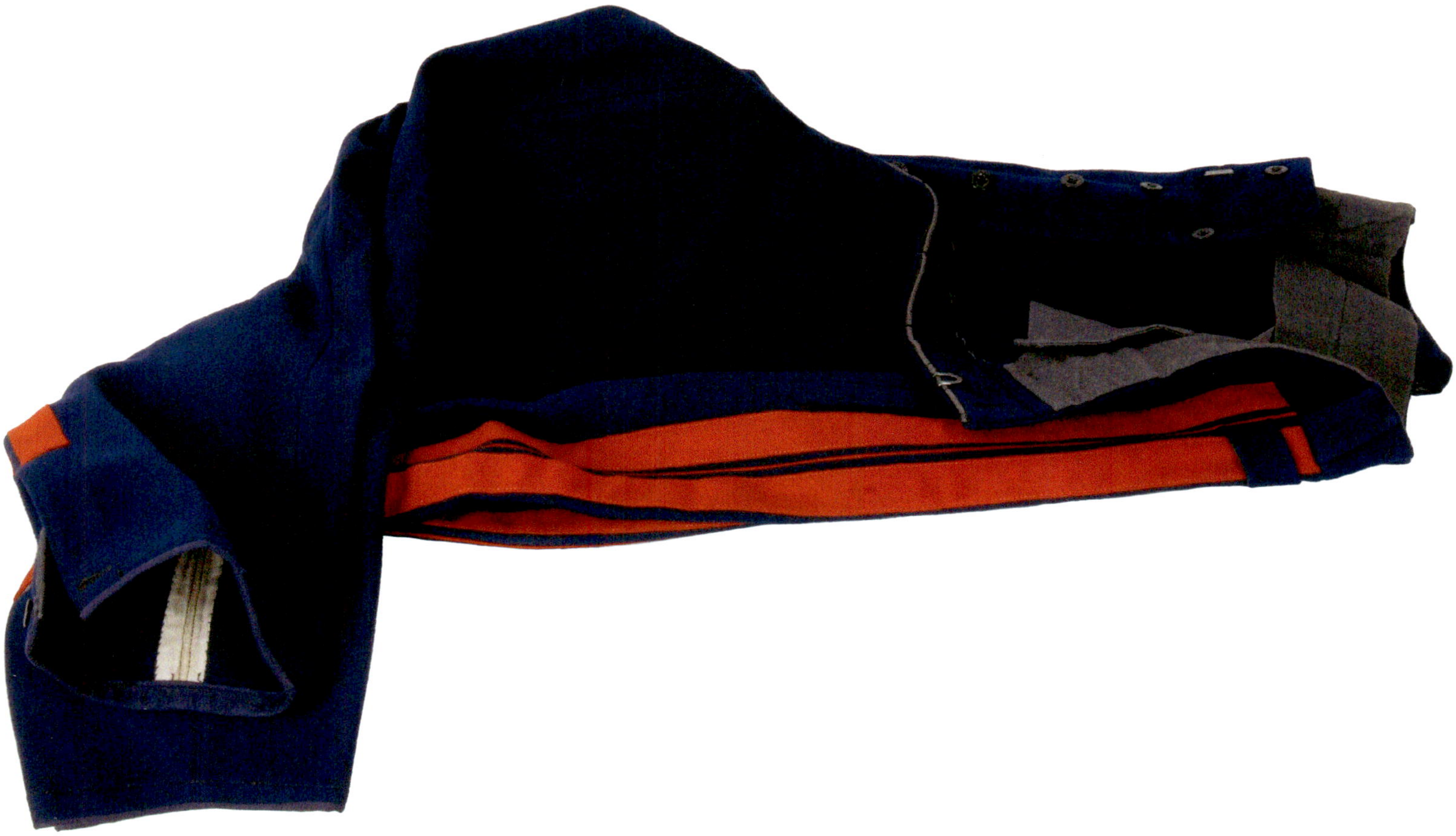

rmy general in his M1943 parade uniform delivering a speech while Commissar Nikita Khrushchev (left) looks on.

A Major General of Artillery in a M1943 Parade Uniform.

CHAPTER TWO

M1943 PARADE UNIFORMS

A great wave of uniform changes took place throughout 1943; perhaps the most striking ensembles were the parade uniforms of the Red Army high command. The January regulation changes kept the grey color of the high command's formal tunics and visor caps, but almost everything else was new. The rank insignia on the collar and cuffs were replaced with the Tsarist-style rank boards and heavy collar embroidery. General's tunic cuffs had three cuff bars or spools, while the branch Marshals' tunic had cuff oak leaf embroidery that matched the collar. The silver belt with red stripes was standard for ranks of Major Generals through Marshals of the USSR.

Marshal of Artillery Nikolai Dmitriyevich Yakovlev in M1943 parade uniform.

M1943 PARADE UNIFORM

OF SOVIET MARSHAL OF ARMORED TROOPS YAKOV NIKOLAYEVICH FEDORENKO

Marshals of Armor and Marshals of Artillery had special collar and cuff coloring reserved for their high ranks. This black velvet backing material on the collar and cuffs was used on both the M1943 parade uniform, as seen here, and on the M1945 uniform. After the war those regulations were struck out. The black velvet was also used on the cap band; this feature today denotes armor.

Another feature unique to branch Marshals was the Marshals' star made of titanium and diamonds, and worn around the neck for both the M1943 and M1945 parade uniforms. There is also evidence that the Marshals' stars were made of gold. This star differed from that worn by Marshal of the USSR in that it lacked the separate diamonds at the inside angles of the star.

Marshal of Armor Yakov Fedorenko's M1943 parade uniform shown here was worn for formal parades until replaced in Spring 1945 by the M1945 parade uniform. Marshal Fedorenko died in 1947.

Marshal of Tanks Yakov N. Fedorenko in his "Victory Parade" uniform.

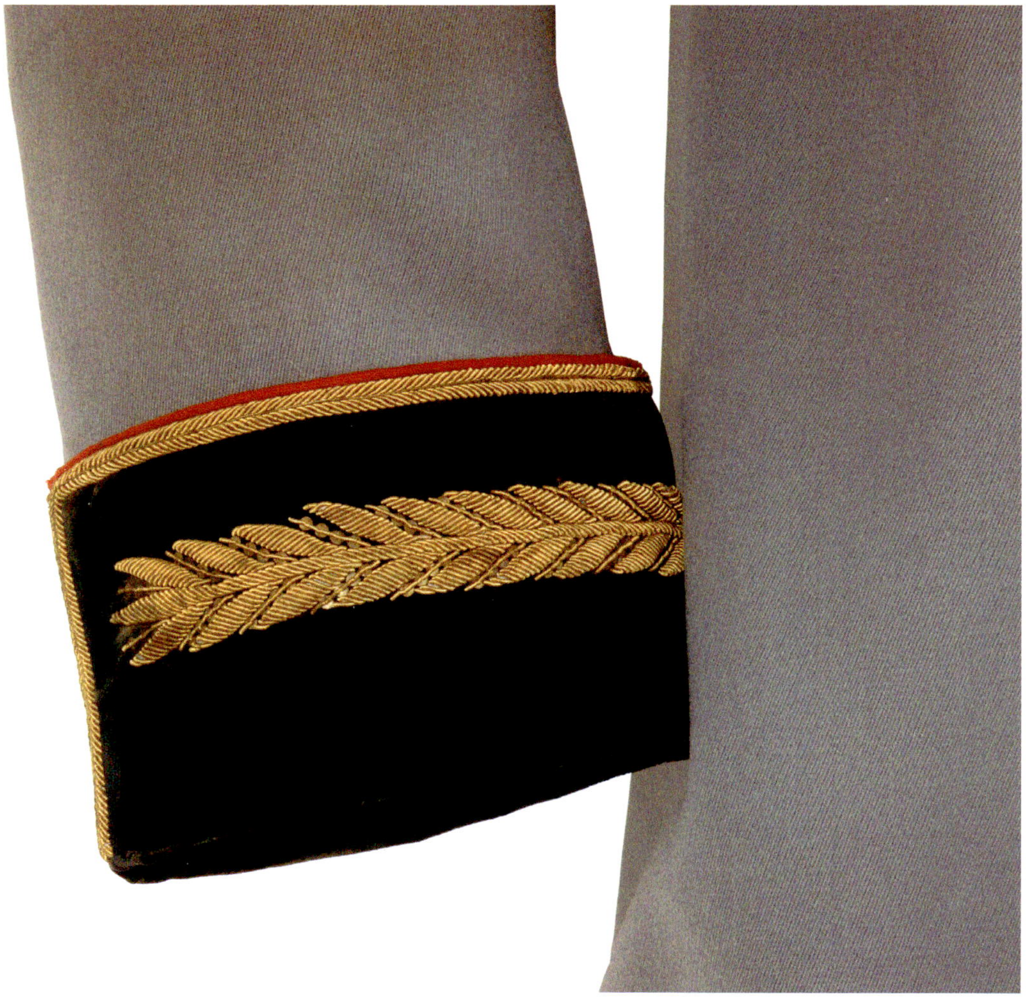

17614
17614

НКЛП МГУЛП РСФСР
Ф-КА
ГОЛОВНЫХ УБОРОВ
N-8
Красный Воин
г. МОСКВА

M1943 PARADE UNIFORM

OF SOVIET AIR MARSHAL
SERGEI ALEXANDROVICH KHUDYAKOV

The Red Air Force high command created the rank of Marshal of Aviation in early 1943. This rank equaled the four-star General in other branches. Eight Red Air Force Generals were given this rank during the Great Patriotic War: Zhavaronkov, Khudyakov, Falaleev, Skripko, Vorozheikin, Astakov, Golavanov, and Novikov. Both Golavanov and Novikov soon achieved the highest rank in the Red Air Force, Chief Marshal of Aviation.

Marshal of Aviation Sergei Khudyakov had a long and, at times, turbulent career. Born Armen Khanferiants in what was Tsarist Armenia, Khudyakov changed his name to honor the man who saved him from drowning during the Russian Civil War. Thus, Sergei Khudyakov was, in a sense, a creation of the revolution!

As many early officers did, Khudyakov started his military career in the cavalry. He later transferred to the still small Red Air Force. A gifted administrator, Khudyakov rose rapidly through the ranks and commanded the air fleets on various fronts; he directed the air power used to defeat the remainder of the Imperial Japanese Army in the Far East. He also served as an advisor on Soviet government policy at the Yalta conference in February 1945.

Unfortunately, Khudyakov's fate was in the hands of the mercurial dictator Joseph Stalin, who had the air Marshal arrested as a British spy and shot on April 18, 1950. Only after Stalin's death was Khudyakov's reputation restored.

When the M1943 rank and uniform revolution occurred, a new full dress parade uniform for branches was created. The single breasted M1943 full dress parade uniform for Marshals of Armor and Artillery was identical to the grey M1943 full dress parade uniform for air Marshals, with heavy gold cuffs and collar embroidery. Rank was also denoted by one large Marshals' rank star. Air Marshals' tunics had the sky blue collars and cuffs of their branch. These collar and cuff colors did not last long after the war, and by the time Colonel-General Vershinin was promoted to air Marshal in 1946, this feature was eliminated. The visor cap retained the standard embroidery of the M1943 and M1945 visor caps for Generals and branch Marshals. Only full Marshals of the USSR had caps with unique Marshal embroidery.

The grey cloth used for both the visor and tunic shown here is lighter weight than that usually found in the full dress parade uniforms for Generals and Marshals. Officers of high rank often had their own tailors make uniforms suitable to their operational theaters' weather. Khudyakov probably had this uniform made for summer use. Medals are worn following the medal and order updates in 1943 which mandated that decorations, such as the Order of Lenin and Order of the Red Banner, be worn on hangers and no longer screwed directly to the uniform. This change was implemented slowly, and often the screw back awards were seen attached to both the M1943 and even M1945 parade uniforms in the old style.

Air Marshal Sergei Alexandrovich Khudyakov in M1943 parade uniform.

Colonel General Konstantin Vershinin in "Victory Parade" uniform. Notice the M1945 parade belt that was issued at the very end of the war with Japan.

Marshal of Armored Troops Pavel Alexeyevich Rotmistrov in M1943 parade uniform.

M1943 PARADE UNIFORM

OF SOVIET MILITIA COMMISSAR 3RD RANK ARTIOM MARKOVICH KUZ'MENKO

The Soviet Police *militsia* forces were under the control of the NKVD, and consequently, their uniforms bore a striking resemblance to the state security forces (Order of the NKVD No.126 from February 1943).

The most ornate of the wartime Soviet police uniforms is the M1943 full dress parade uniform for "Comissars" of the Red Police. The title Comissar was equivalent to the military General. The uniform's silver cuff and collar embroidery denotes a non-combat role.

The tunic itself is a very high-quality, deep-blue wool with state security blue piping and special NKVD point cuff embroidery; blue Comissar stripes are woven into the shoulder boards.

The visor cap patterned after the tunic is of rich, blue wool, with state security piping and silver embroidery. The hat uses the standard M1940 Red Army General officers' cap badge, even though regulations called for a special militia Comissar's badge. Scarcity and expediency forced the use of the army badge more often than not.

The tunic is decorated with the pre-1943 Order of Lenin and the distinguished service in the NKVD badge.

This is the first of four uniforms that came out of the Ukraine belonging to Soviet Militia Commissar 3rd Rank Artiom Kuz'menko. Commissar Kuz'menko spent his career in the Soviet security service in the Ukraine. His postings included being a top militia officer in Zhitomir, Nikolaev, and Odessa. Commissar Kuz'menko died in 1995.

Militia Commissar 3rd Rank Artiom Markovich Kuz'menko.

Photo showing an air officer (left) and a NKGB officer in a rare lapelled uniform with Commissar Khrushchev (right).

M1943 PARADE UNIFORM

OF A SOVIET VICE ADMIRAL

The Red Navy high command included Admirals and Generals of special services. From 1943 forward, Admirals of the Red Navy, like those of the Tsarist navy, had cuff rank denoted by gold bars and shoulder boards with one to four stars. Admirals had sleeve ranks that corresponded with western naval forces. The M1943 full dress parade uniform shown here, of a vice Admiral, displays the matching shoulder and cuff rank, the double-breasted tunic, and the heavy gold collar embroidery. This cut and extra embroidery were changed for the M1945 parade uniforms. The M1943 service uniforms did not change in 1945.

This vice Admiral wears his full dress parade M1943 tunic with the dress belt in silk cloth, rather than the more common brocade gold. His visor cap is the standard M1943 parade and service cap; Admirals did not get a specialized parade visor cap until 1945.

M1943 PARADE UNIFORM

OF A SOVIET LIEUTENANT GENERAL OF NAVAL ADMINISTRATION

The Red Navy was a large and intricate organization that required specialists in many non-combat related careers, such as legal and medical. The top commanders in these branches wore uniforms similar to their combat counterparts, but with some important differences.

The most striking and apparent difference was in the color of the shoulder board's metallic backing. While the boards were decorated in gold for Generals and Admirals who had combat commands, the color of the boards for both the service and parade uniforms for administrative commanders was silver.

The silver insignia, silver belt, and red piping on this Red Navy Lieutenant General's uniform indicates his service in administration. The lack of specialty legal or medical insignia on the boards of this high ranking officer indicates he was an administrative naval General.

The M1943 parade uniform, standard for Generals of the Red Navy, has three cuff bars instead of the traditional naval rank stripes used for Red Navy Admirals. The Order of the Red Star and an Order of the Red Banner of Labor adorn this uniform. High ranking administrative officials with labor, rather than combat, awards were common.

As the war came to a close in 1945, the 1943 and 1945 uniforms were often mixed and matched as a result of war shortages and changing priorities. This Lieutenant General has already received his M1945 full dress parade visor with correct silver embroidery, but his matching tunic is not yet complete.

Admiral Ivan Sepanovich Yumashev in dress whites uniform.

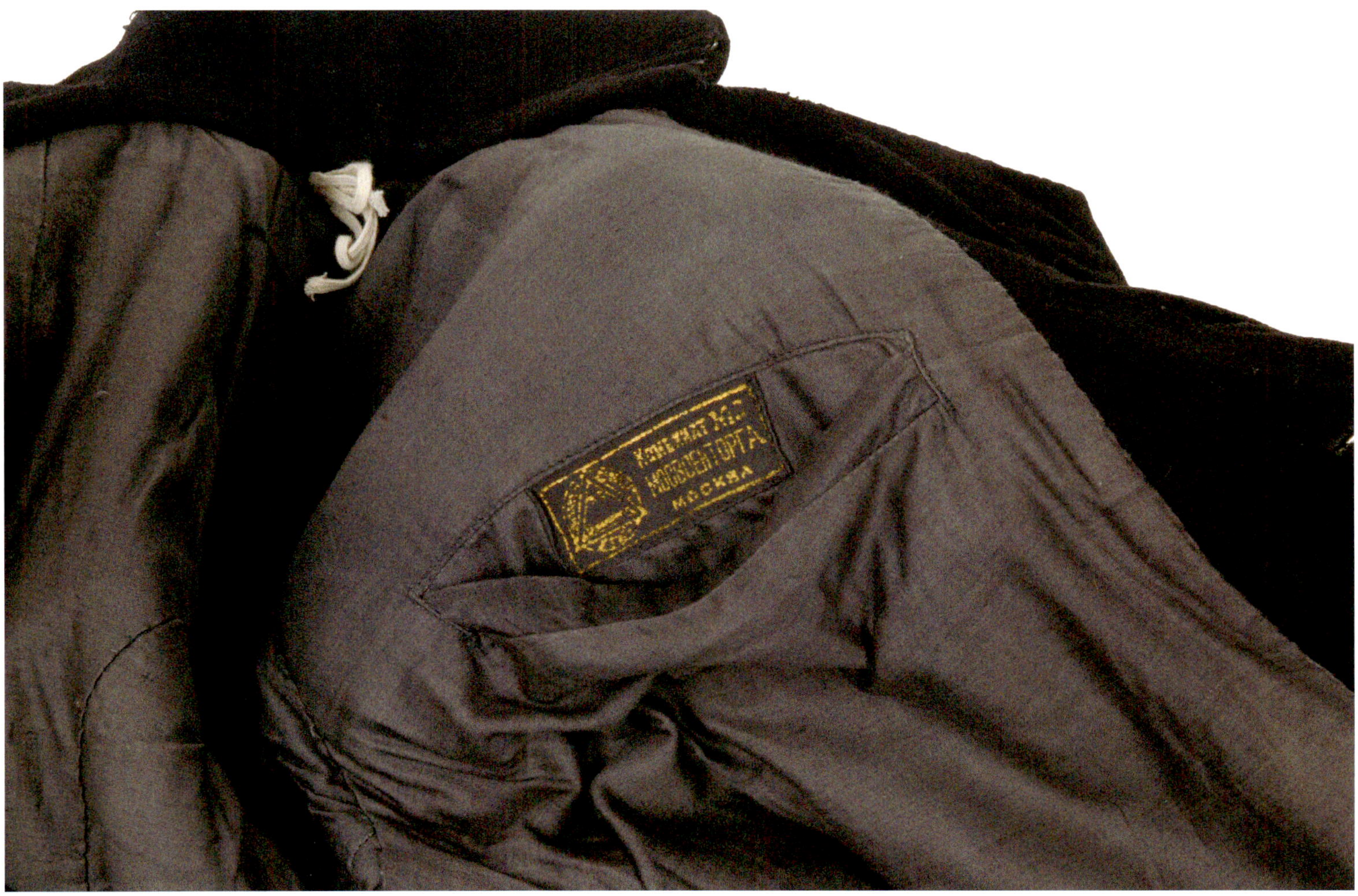
МОСВОЕНТОРГА
МОСКВА

Field Marshal Bernard L. Montgomery and Marshal of the Soviet Union Konstantin Rokossovsky with staff officers after their link-up in the Baltic Sea area, May 7, 1945.

A NKVD Major General and two members of his staff in service uniforms.

CHAPTER THREE

M1943 SERVICE, DRESS WHITE UNIFORMS AND OVERCOATS

Major General Daniil Ivanovich Esipenko in a M1943 service uniform. A NKVD badge is worn on his pocket.

M1943 SERVICE UNIFORM

OF SOVIET MILITIA COMMISSAR 3RD RANK ARTIOM MARKOVICH KUZ'MENKO

In the early postwar years, Commissar Kuz'menko wore this everyday service, M1943 style, tunic that paralleled the design of the new parade uniform: dark blue wool with red piping on the collar and cuffs, and silver boards with no Comissar stripes. This basic uniform design remained the template of the Soviet police leadership for the rest of USSR history. Pictured here is the tunic with the full parade version of the visor cap for a more formal, though not full parade, event. The standard cap for this tunic had no embroidery.

A war time photograph showing a Major General and his family. The younger soldier on the right is a Junior Lieutenant of Artillery.

M1943 SUMMER DRESS WHITE UNIFORM

OF SOVIET MILITIA COMMISSAR 3RD RANK ARTIOM MARKOVICH KUZ'MENKO

This wartime M1943 Summer mundir of Commissar Kuz'menko shows the striped *militsia* boards. Other than the boards, this tunic is identical to the version used by Generals in the Red Army and Air Force. Commissar Kuz'menko's summer tunic is pictured with his dress visor cap. Often the addition of a parade cap to the summer dress whites was used for occasions requiring more formality. Officers wore dress whites in the office, on the parade field, and at high-level conferences.

Marshal of the Soviet Union Georgy Konstantinovich Zhukov wearing a dress whites uniform.

M1943 SUMMER DRESS WHITE UNIFORM

OF A COLONEL GENERAL JUDGE OF THE SOVIET ARMY

When the 1943 uniform regulation changes came into effect, officers from Lieutenant through Marshal of the USSR were to have a white summer service tunic. In practice, most non-flag-rank officers did not receive a white tunic. The war dictated other priorities. The higher ranking Red Army command, however, had the ability to make sure they had the summer uniforms.

The M1943 white summer service tunic fabric for flag-rank officers varied from wool (an odd choice for summer) to linen, cotton, or even silk. The tunic had two chest pockets with no piping on the collar and cuffs.

The silk example shown here, with three stars on silver boards and judicial insignia, is for a Colonel-General of the legal service, or more accurately an army lawyer, the highest rank for the judicial corps. Two stars indicated a corps military lawyer; a single star denoted a divisional military lawyer.

While the silver boards show this very high ranking officer to be a non-combatant, the narrow width of the boards shows that his position was appointed, and he was most likely assigned his rank during the war.

In all likelihood, this military lawyer was a top-ranking judge in the Red Army.

A Vice Admiral confers with a fellow officer, both of whom are wearing service uniforms.

Major General Alexander Kotikov wearing a M1943 service uniform. This photo dates to 1950, showing that these uniforms were worn well after the end of World War II.

Marshal of the Soviet Union Konstantin Rokossovsky meeting with officers towards the end of the war. He is shown facing the camera wearing a M1943 service uniform with a leather cross belt.

M1943 RAINCOAT

OF MARSHAL OF THE SOVIET UNION KLIMENT YEFREMOVICH VOROSHILOV

The 1943 uniform regulation changes that overhauled the insignia and rank of the Red Army encompassed all forms of issued clothing. The M1943 overcoat and raincoat for general officers were of similar design, but differed in material weight. M1943 rank boards replaced the collar and cuff rankings, and a special, single-button collar tab was added for the collar. The General's specialty determined the branch color of these tabs. Marshals of the USSR wore red tabs. These tabs would eventually show up again on the 1945 service tunic for the Generalissimus of the USSR.

The example shown here is worn over the M1945 "Victory Parade" uniform for Marshal of the USSR Voroshilov. It has red collar tabs and the standard rank boards for Marshal of the USSR. Under the coat, this Marshal wears his medals and the very rare M1945 gold dress belt with an extra support hanger cross strap that carried the M1940 dress saber's weight.

M1943 OVERCOAT

OF MARSHAL OF TANKS PAVEL ALEXEYEVICH ROTMISTROV

It has been said that the fist of the conquering Red Army was the armored forces. The masses of T-34s and scattered I-S2 "Stalin" heavy tanks that rolled through Russia and Eastern Europe crushed the Wehrmacht, at one time the strongest army in the world.

The commanders of these armored formations were rewarded with orders, medals, and high rank. The highest of these ranks, instituted in February 1943 as part of the sweeping uniform rank and insignia change, was Marshal of Armor. The ranks of Marshal of Artillery and Marshal of Aviation were also adopted. Marshal of Engineering and Marshal of Signals were not adopted until October 1943. The rank of Senior Marshal, sometimes called Chief Marshal of Armor, was adopted in late 1943, but it was not actually awarded until 1962.

The rank insignia for Marshal of Armor was a single large embroidered Marshals' star and tank outline. Pictured here is a M1943 overcoat attributed to Marshal of Tanks Pavel Rotmistrov. Both artillery and armor wore boards with black collar tabs. The overcoat is piped in red with two rows of six buttons. The lapel can be worn open or closed. The red piping on the cuffs, front, and pockets indicates that this overcoat is for formal or parade use. The overcoat style remained unchanged for the remainder of the war.

Marshal of Armored Troops Pavel Alexeyevich Rotmistrov wearing a M1943 overcoat.

Alexander Pokryshkin (left), Marshal of the Soviet Union Georgy Konstantinovich Zhukov, and Ivan Kozhedub – the "Ace of Aces," who had 62 air victories during the war – each wearing three Hero of the Soviet Union awards.

Marshal of the USSR Ivan Stepanovich Konev and another general wearing their M1943 overcoats.

Portrait of Marshal of the Soviet Union Georgy Konstantinovich Zhukov wearing his highly decorated "Victory Parade" uniform. Part of the Sinclair collection, this is a 1976 copy of the original painting that was done in 1945.

CHAPTER FOUR

M1945 VICTORY PARADE UNIFORMS

A photo taken in 1945 of troops at the "Victory Parade," showing Soviet soldiers draping the flags of the defeated enemy on the ground.

M1945 WALKING OUT DRESS UNIFORM

OF GENERALISSIMUS OF THE SOVIET UNION JOSEF VISSARIONOVICH STALIN

The term *generalissimo* has been used throughout history to represent the highest military leader, such as *Generalissimo* Francisco Franco of Spain and *Generalissimo* Chiang Kai-shek of China. The term itself in the original Italian means the highest General, and is often used as a title rather than a rank.

However, in the Soviet military hierarchy the term *Generalissimus* of the Soviet Union is an actual rank higher than Marshal of the USSR, and implies both overall command of the Red Army and Commander in Chief of the Armed Forces. The rank was created on June 26, 1945, for Joseph Stalin, who had held the ranks of Marshal of the USSR and Commander in Chief of the Soviet Armed Forces. While the rank description did not specify that the title could only be awarded to Stalin, all understood the rank was created for him. Joseph Stalin is the only person to have been promoted from Marshal of the USSR to *Generalissimus* of the Soviet Union in USSR history.

The insignia for this highest of Soviet ranks, although never implemented, had a new design concept based on the insignia for Marshal of the USSR. One design included embellishments, such as laurel wreaths surrounding the large rank star to differentiate the Supreme Marshal of the USSR in the same way that supreme branch Marshals' rank laurel wreaths differentiated them from branch Marshals. In the end, even with quite a few new prototypes designed and produced, the eventual *Generalissimus* uniform would retain the traditional Marshal of the USSR boards.

The M1943 and M1945 parade uniforms and the M1943 service uniforms for Marshals of the Soviet Union and *Generalissimus* of the Soviet Union were often identical. Immediately after Stalin was photographed wearing the new M1943 parade uniform, he had his secretary send the uniform to the Central Armed Forces Museum with a note saying that he didn't care to wear it again. In 1945, when the "Victory Parade" uniforms were being designed, a longer frock coat with fringed epaulets was made especially for him, but Stalin refused to wear it. The only unique uniform for the rank *Generalissimus* was the M1945 dress uniform. The tunic, which ironically enough was originally Tsarist in design, had a five-button front with a turned-down collar. It was rumored that Stalin found the traditional stand-up collar of the M1943 service uniform to be uncomfortable. Red wool or cotton tabs, surrounded on three sides by gold thread embroidery unique to the rank of *Generalissimus*, decorated the collar. At the top of the collar tab was a flag rank button sewn into the tab itself. These collar tabs were used on overcoats and raincoats for Generals and Marshals, but not on their tunics. The shoulder rank insignia of *Generalissimus* of the USSR was identical to that of Marshal of the USSR, with the large embroidered star along with the state seal of the Soviet Union on gold thread.

The material of the *Generalissimus* uniform varied. The material pictured here is rainbow denim. Heavier and darker grey wool and white cotton were also used.

After Stalin's death in 1953, the head of the USSR, while not actually holding any military rank, was considered Commander in Chief of the Soviet Armed Forces.

Marshal Stalin wearing a M1945 marshal's "Victory Parade" cap.

A portrait of Nicholas II by Valentin Aleksandrovich Serov. Notice the similarities between the Tsar's and Stalin's uniform.

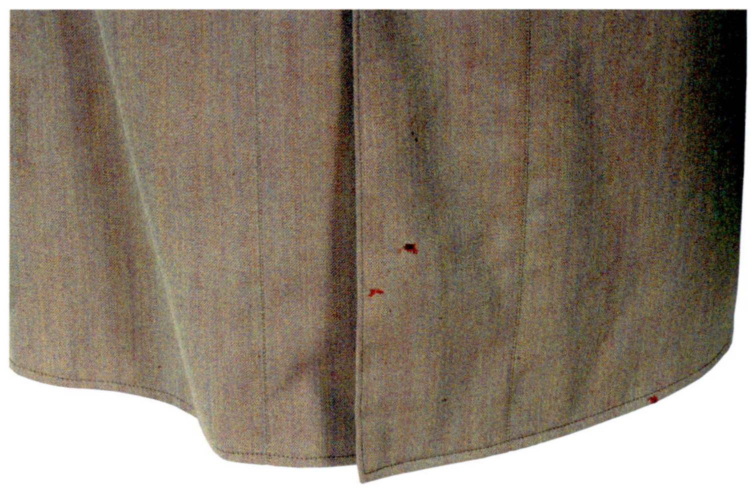

367
367

Postwar official state portrait of Premir Josef Stalin.

Russian and American gift swap in Germany. Gifts are exchanged by leaders of victorious American and Russian forces during a gala get-together May 5, 1945, celebrating the capitulation of the Nazis. At top, Omar N. Bradley of the U.S. 12th Army Group, pets the beautiful steed present to him by Russian Marshal Ivan Konev. In the lower photograph, General Bradley hands Marshal Konev an American Army carbine. The jeep in the foreground is another gift from the Americans to the Russians.

Original portrait of Marshal Zhukov. This was painted in 1945 by Pavel Korin (1892-1967). Notice that the original portrait has Marshal Zhukov wearing three Hero of the Soviet Union stars, while the later portrait has the fourth star, awarded December 1, 1956, painted in. It was common practice to add awards to paintings and to uniforms on display in museums, even though the awards were bestowed years later or even posthumously.

Official State photograph of Marshal of the Soviet Union Zhukov in his "Victory Parade" uniform.

Official photograph of Marshal of the Soviet Union Fyodor Ivanovich Tolbukhin (1892-1949) wearing his "Victory Parade" uniform.

Marshal of the Soviet Union Rodion Yakovlevich Malinovsky (1898-1967)
in "Victory Parade" attire.

Marshal Stalin and Marshal of the Soviet Union Semen Mikhailovich Budenny converse while taking a walk in Moscow. They are followed at a safe distance by their entourage.

M1945 VICTORY PARADE UNIFORM

OF A SOVIET MARSHAL OF ARMORED TROOPS

In April 1945, victory seemed only weeks away, and the Red Army high command changed the parade uniform regulations. This new uniform was simply called the "Victory Parade" uniform, because of its debut at the victory parade in Moscow on June 24, 1945. Stalin used this new uniform as a propaganda tool to visually display that the Soviet Union was now a world power with the strength and resources to prove it.

The "Victory Parade" uniform had both a striking double-breasted, Tsarist-like design and a rich peacock blue-green color. This is perhaps the most beautiful of all the Soviet uniforms, and is considered by many to be the most beautiful uniform of World War II.

While the M1945 parade uniforms for Marshals of Armor received the update in color and cut, they retained some of the unique qualities of the M1943 parade uniform. The black velvet collar, cuffs, and hat band would ensure that Armor Marshals would stand out in the sea of Red Army commanders at parades.

While the silver M1943 parade belt was used at the first victory parade, Generals and Marshals wore a new gold dress belt for victory parades held later in 1945, and indeed for the rest of the Soviet era, with only minor changes.

The Marshal of Armor uniform shown here, with the gold belt, indicates that it was worn later in 1945. The black collar, cuffs, and cap badge are striking against the color and double-breasted, imperial cut of the tunic.

The rank of Marshal of Armor was not equivalent to Marshal of the USSR; it was on the same level as a four-star General of the army. Only four men achieved this rank in World War II: Pavel Rotmistrov, Yakov Fedorenko, Semyan Bogdanov, and Pavel Rybalko. Rotmistrov and Fedorenko were awarded the rank in early 1944, while Rybalko and Bogdanov followed a few months later. Only two men were appointed to this rank in the postwar years: Mikhail Katukov and Hamazap Babadzhanian.

Twice Hero of the Soviet Union Marshal of Armored Troops Pavel Semjonovich Rybalko (1892-1948).

ЛЕНИН
ЛЕНИН

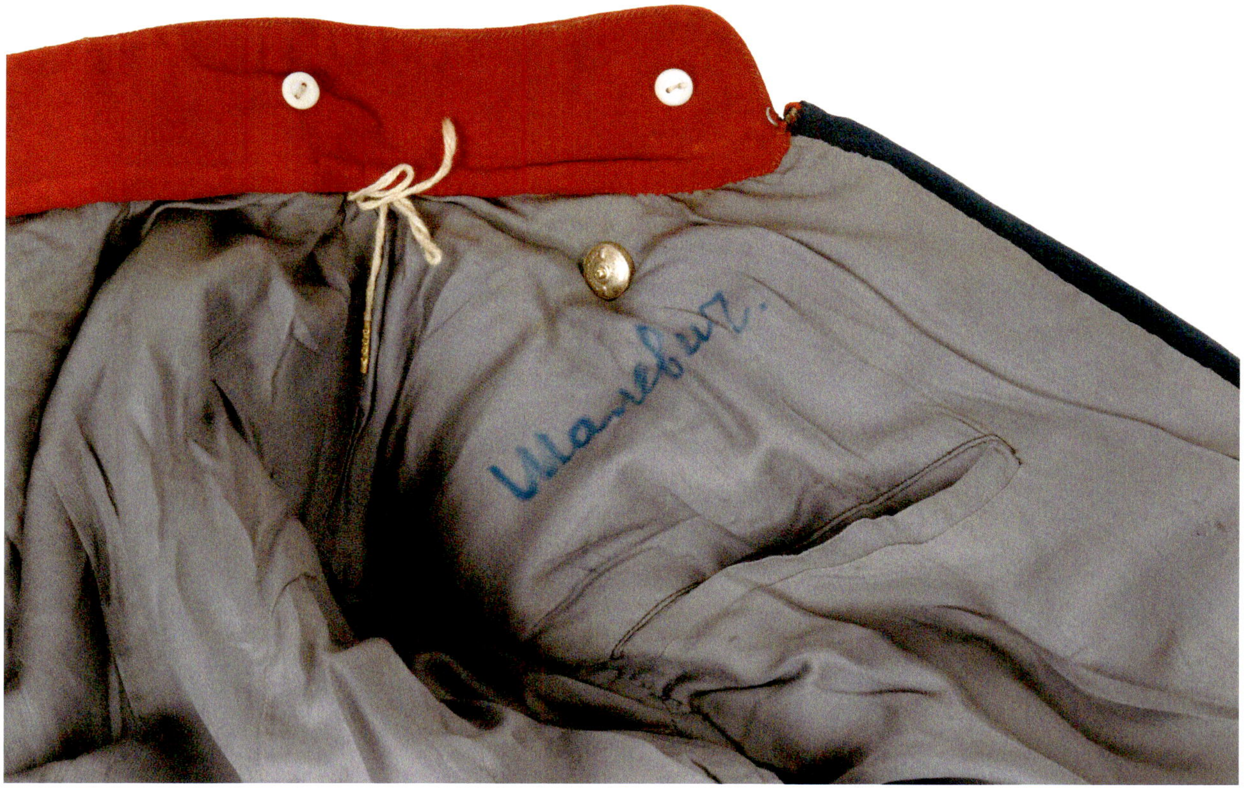

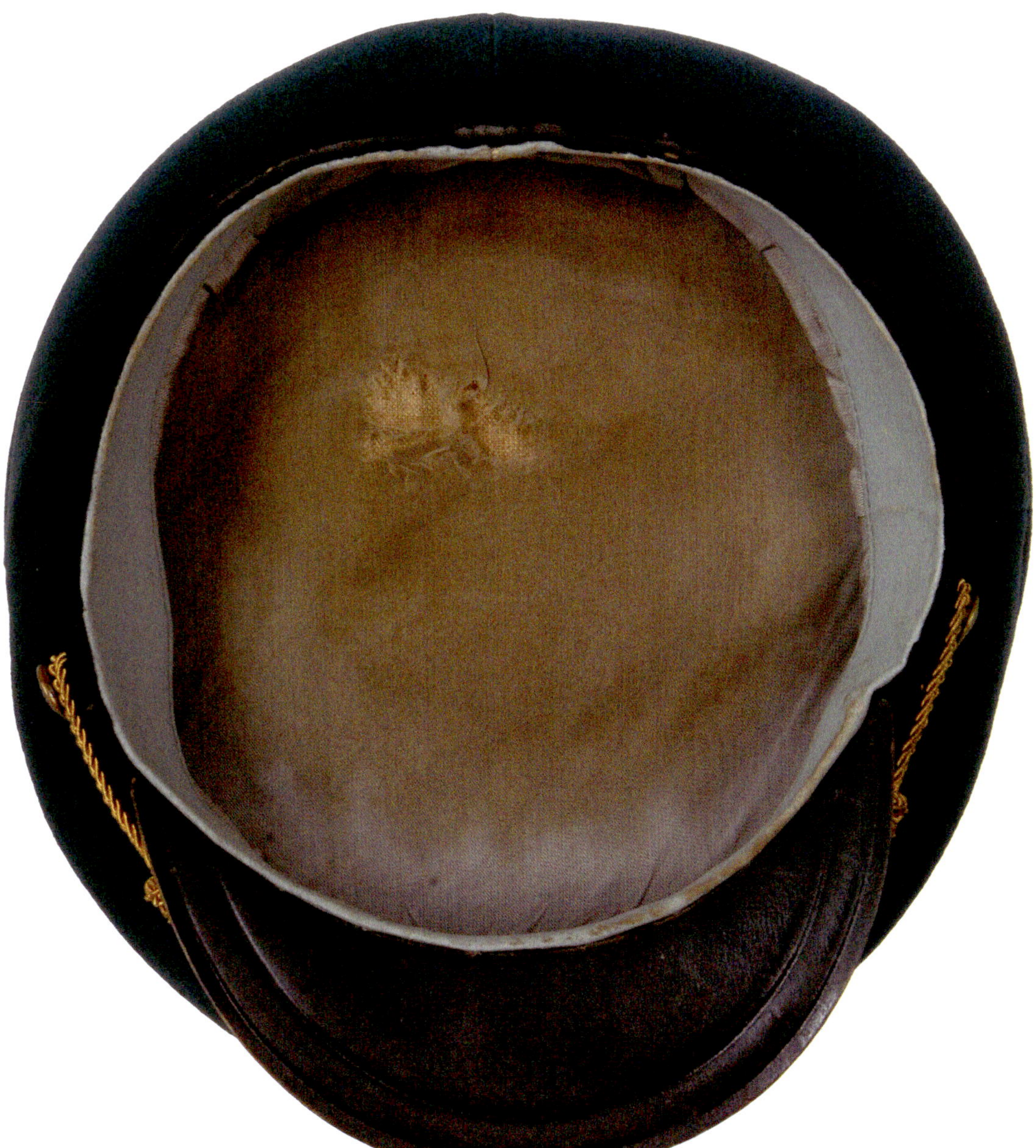

Marshal of Armored Troops Semon Iliich Bogdanov (1894-1960) wearing two Hero of the Soviet Union stars.

Air Marshal Aleksander Aleksandrovich Novikov in his M1945 "Victory Parade" Uniform. Notice the Legion of Merit breast badge awarded to him by the Allies at the end of the war.

A photograph of an unidentified Lieutenant General.

A General mounted on a horse waits in a "Victory Parade" procession. There was some resistance at first by some high ranking officers, including Marshal Zhukov, to riding horses. Some of the officers didn't feel comfortable on a horse. Marshal Stalin insisted that this was what he wanted, and his wishes prevailed.

M1945 "VICTORY PARADE UNIFORM"

OF GENERAL OF THE ARMY
MAXSIM ALEKSEYEVICH PURKAEV

Perhaps the most attractive uniforms ever produced by the USSR, and reminiscent of the Tsarist past, were those for the parades at the end of the Great Patriotic War. A full description of the design, manufacture, and use of the M1945 "Victory Parade" uniforms can be found in Volume I of *World War II Parade Uniforms of the Soviet Union*.

The highest rank for officers in the Red Army, before the senior rank of Marshal of the USSR, was that of General of the Army. Except for the number of stars on the shoulder boards, the M1945 uniforms for this rank were identical for all ranks of Generals. The rank for General of the Army was designated with four silver embroidered stars.

The uniform pictured here was worn by General of the Army Maxsim Alekseyevich Purkaev, who after 1943 was one of the top Red Army commanders in the Far East.

General of the Army Purkaev had been one of only a handful of Tsarist officers who was able to make the transition into the new Red Army at the outbreak of the Russian Civil War in 1918 and still rise to a top command. Purkaev showed a strong command of military tactics and was sent to Red Army Officers' Command School at the end of the civil war.

Purkaev was the Soviet military attaché in Berlin in1939, and was a key liaison officer between the Red Army and the *Wehrmacht* in the planning of the occupation and division of Poland.

Throughout the Great Patriotic War, Purkaev served in various staff appointments. At the latter part of the war he was sent to command the Far Eastern Front, and later, the Second Far Eastern Front against Japan.

Purkaev served as head of the higher education section of the Soviet army from 1947 until his death in 1953.

Although he did not earn the top honor of Hero of the Soviet Union, General of the Army Purkaev was well-decorated and had been awarded two Orders of Lenin, an Order of Suvorov First Class, and an Order of Kutuzov First Class.

State Portrait of General of the Army Maksim Alekseyevich Purkaev (1894-1953).

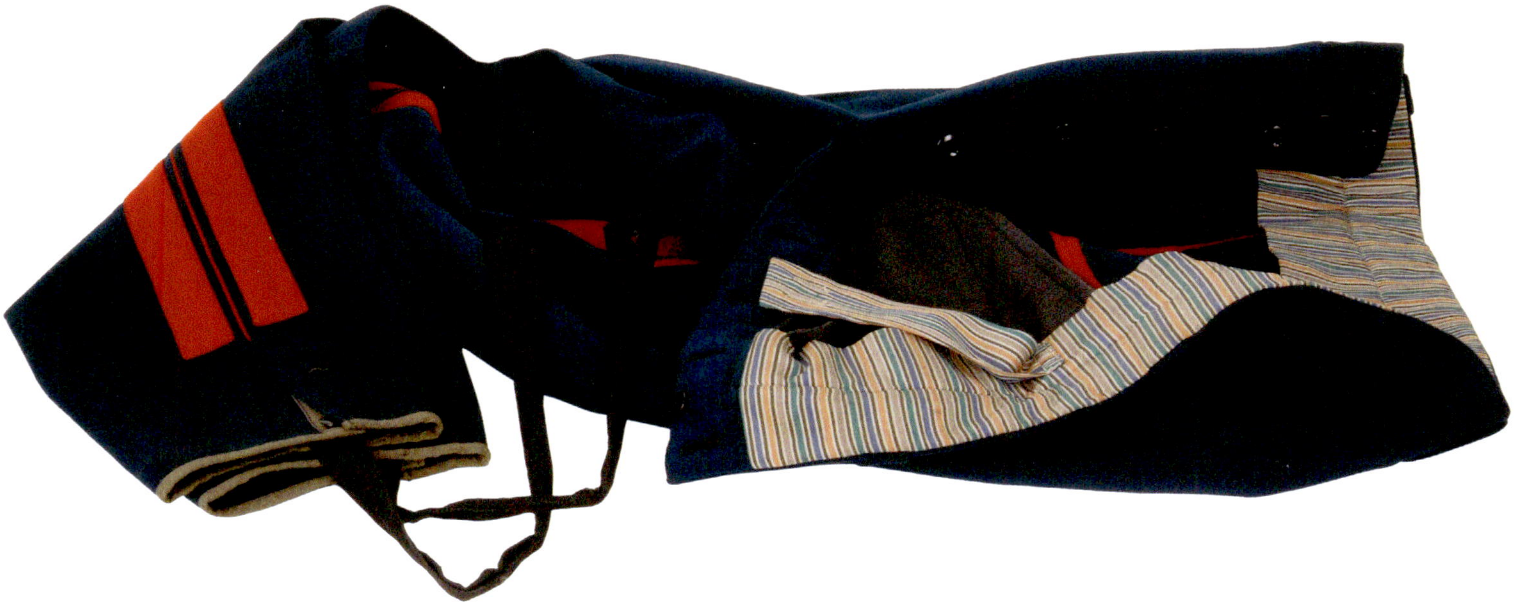

Major General A. P. Kislenko and his wife at a diplomatic reception.

Photograph of an unidentified Major General of Artillery

M1945 "Victory Parade Uniform"

Photograph of an unidentified Major General.

A photograph of an unidentified Guards Major General

An unidentified Guards Lieutenant General.

An unidentified Major General.

M1945 "VICTORY PARADE"

UNIFORM OF SOVIET MILITIA COMMISSAR 3RD RANK ARTIOM MARLOVICH KUZ'MENKO

After the war, Commissar Kuz'menko kept his high rank, but the militia received new uniforms. The NKVD became the MGB and the MVD, and the *militsia* was placed under MVD control. The use of the single-breasted M1943 parade uniform was followed by its "Victory Parade," double-breasted, dark blue replacement (MVD Order No.553 September 1947). Red piping replaced the blue piping, a color scheme that would last until the end of the USSR.

The special Comissar stripes on the shoulder boards were removed, but the color of the boards, collar, and cuff embroidery remained silver. The cap material matches the dark blue color of the tunic. The special Commissar of the *Militsia* cap badge is done with the USSR state seal in heavy brass.

The belt pictured, made of gold rather than silver brocade, is the correct M1943 full-dress belt worn with this uniform.

The medal bar is a semi-representative example of what Commissar Kuz'menko would have worn. Besides the Order of Lenin, he was awarded the Defense of Stalingrad and the Defense of Odessa medals.

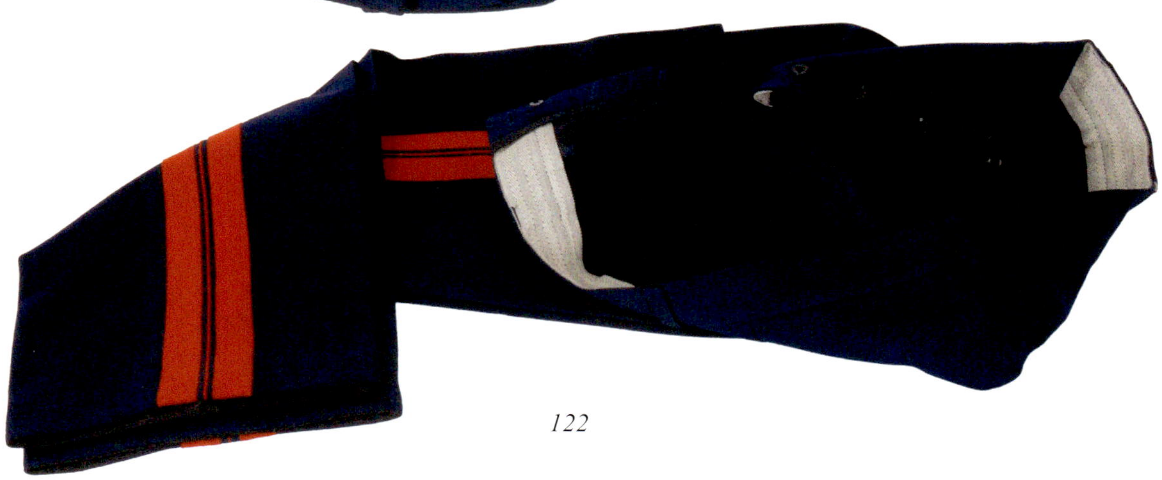

M1945 "VICTORY PARADE"

UNIFORM OF NKVD-MGB TRANSPORTATION UNITS COLONEL GENERAL

SERGEI ARSENTEVICH GOGLIDZE

From the beginning of the new communist state, the structure of the Soviet security services was varied and complicated. The internal security, rifle troops, frontier troops, and intelligence all had their own mission, command structure, and senior staff. During the Second World War, all of these branches would eventually end up reporting to Lavrenti Beria, the head of the entire Soviet security apparatus.

Many NKVD officers served in multiple branches of service during their careers. Assignment changes commonly moved an officer from the frontier troops to internal troops, or vice versa. Colonel General Sergei Arsentevich Goglidze was a prominent example of an officer who made many of these transitions. Goglidze began in the 1920s with the new frontier troops of the USSR. He eventually moved up through the ranks and found his way into the more powerful and prestigious internal affairs service. He later served in Leningrad and Georgia as an officer in the NKVD internal affairs branch. Goglidze then served in the Far East with the NKGB, the state security branch of the NKVD.

After the Great Patriotic War, Colonel General Goglidze was made head of the MGB directorate of security of railways and waterways, the transport security. The striking color combinations of the black uniform with crimson piping and gold embroidery of the transport security uniforms evoke Tsarist regulations. (See the uniform of Major General Makaraeyev in Volume I of *World War II Parade Uniforms of the Soviet Union*.)

Colonel General Goglidze, the only officer to hold the three-star rank in this branch, did not hold this position for long. He was arrested and shot in 1953.

Colonel General Serghei Arsentevich Goglidze.

Marshal Stalin and Ambassador of the Soviet Diplomatic Corps Andre Yanoravich Vishinsky (far left with glasses) at the Yalta Conference, which took place February 4 to 11, 1945. President Roosevelt is seen on the right just weeks before his death. Prime Minister Winston Churchill is in the lower right of the photo.

A photograph of an unidentified Major General with his wife and son.

Troops parading their banner in the field.

M1945 "VICTORY PARADE" UNIFORM

OF A COLONEL GENERAL OF THE RED AIR FORCE

By the end of the Great Patriotic War, the Red Air Force had regained control of the skies over the USSR and Eastern Europe. The air units supported the massive ground campaign that moved forward to capture German territory, destroy the German armed forces, and ultimately, to raise the red banner over Berlin.

The high command of the Red Air Force was dominated by the Air Marshals. Directly under the Air Marshals were the Colonel Generals, who were the commanders of the aviation fronts and large numbers of aircraft and airmen; they reported directly to the Red Air Force high command. In the postwar years, many of them rose to the highest ranks of the Red Air Force: Marshal of Aviation and Senior Marshal of Aviation.

The M1945 uniform here for a Colonel General of the Red Air Force is very similar to the example found on page 235 of Volume I of this series. The slight difference is mostly due to simple preference. The example shown here has a higher and more ornate collar, smaller cuffs, and more widely spaced leaf embroidery on the visor cap. Although the M1945 uniform had a standard design, there were subtle differences for each tailored example.

Colonel General of the NKVD Victor Semenovich Abakumov (right) was arrested and executed as a traitor in 1954.

M1945 "VICTORY PARADE"

UNIFORM OF A SOVIET REAR ADMIRAL OF ENGINEERING

The engineering branches in both the Red Army and Red Navy are considered combat or line service. A great deal of respect was given to these engineers, both on land and at sea, and they often rose to the highest ranks. The Red Army had its own Marshal of Engineering. In the Red Navy, engineers rose through the ranks like regular line officers all the way to three-star Admirals. The uniforms for engineering admirals and line admirals were identical: a set of crossed wrenches on the M1943 boards indicated the specialty.

This example of a rear Admiral of engineer's M1945 "Victory Parade" uniform is standard for the ranks of Rear Admiral through full Admiral. The engineering insignia is identical to the M1943 Rear Admiral's parade boards, shown on page 60 in Volume I of this compendium.

M1945 "VICTORY PARADE" UNIFORM

OF A SOVIET MAJOR GENERAL OF NAVAL AVIATION

The aviators of the USSR served in both the Red Air Force and the naval aviation branch. Although the USSR lacked any sort of aircraft carrier, the navy controlled considerable air assets.

The high command of soviet naval aviation was, like the regular Red Air Force, made up of generals. The lowest of these ranks, indicated with a single star on the shoulder boards, was that of Major General. Soviet generals of naval aviation had uniforms that mixed elements of both the Red Air Force, such as rank insignia, and the Red Navy, such as the tunic itself.

The uniform shown here illustrates a combination of branch insignia. The M1945 "Victory Parade" tunic is the same basic uniform for all Red Navy Admirals and Generals. The uniforms of naval aviation generals had sky-blue piping, while naval admirals had black piping that blended in with the rest of the tunic. Both uniforms had identical gold embroidery on the collar, but different embroidery on the cuffs. Admirals retained the three anchor insignia on the cuffs; generals of all naval branches wore three cuff spools. The shoulder boards are the same as those worn by regular generals of the Red Air Force. The M1945 parade visor cap was standard for both naval generals and admirals. The M1940 brocade belt shown here has the somewhat more rare lion heads on the hangers.

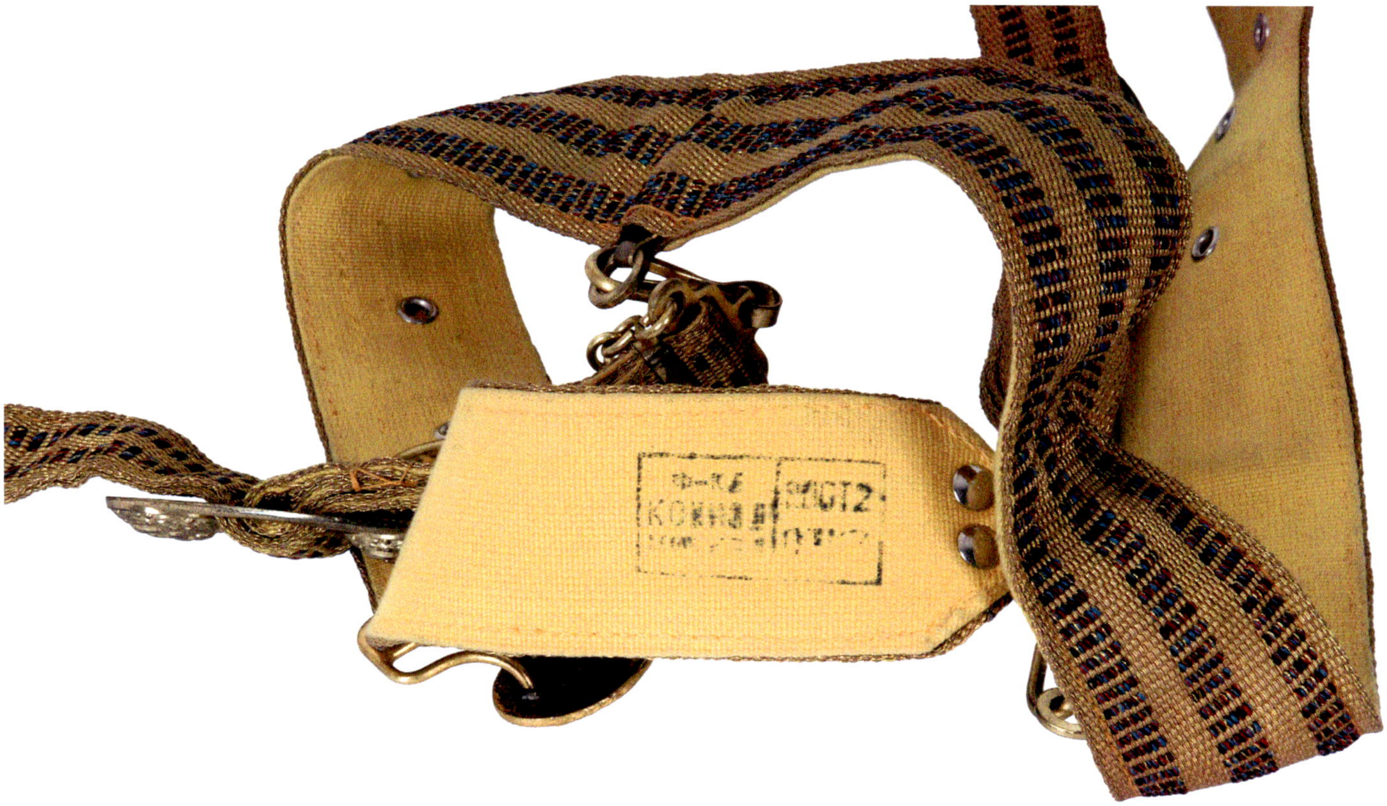

A NKVD Naval Counter Intelligence Lieutenant General.

Russian generals on their way across the Elbe River to visit Ninth Army Headquarters, May 31, 1945. L-R: Lieutenant General Victor K. Urbanovich, Lieutenant General Makar V. Ivashechkin, Major General Ivan D. Pinchuk, Colonel General Alexander V. Gorbatov, Commanding General 3rd Russian Army, and Lieutenant General Peter P. Sobennikov. This photograph was taken by Tec 4 Elmer Allen, U.S. Army Signal Corps.

An unidentified Major General.

An unidentified Major General.

An unidentified Major General.

An unidentified Lieutenant General.

M1940 NKVD

ENGRAVED GENERAL OFFICERS DRESS SABER

The saber has a long history in Russia that stretches from the early Tsarist officer corps to the rebellious Cossacks, who carried curved sabers called *shashkas*. From the revolution until 1940, the saber had a field use for cavalry units, but lacked the parade use it had under the Tsar.

The Tsarist-style M1943 uniform changes didn't come until halfway through the war, but, ironically enough, the use of a bright chrome parade saber came in 1940, right before the outbreak of the Great Patriotic War.

The M1940 saber for general officers was designed for marshals and generals of "troops of the line," such as rifles, artillery and, of course, cavalry. Generals of other branches wore the M1940 long dress dagger.

The saber itself is made up of a steel blade with a wooden handle and a chromed scabbard. The fittings are also chromed.

This particular example, belonging to a NKVD general, had a professional engraving added in 1975 for the 30th Anniversary of Victory, and, later, a less professional engraving done by the General himself as he passed the saber "from father to son."

The saber, when first used in 1940, was hung from leather hangers worn with the leather dress belt. In both 1943 and 1945, the saber was held by hangers made from the same brocade material as the M1943 parade belt. In 1945, the saber was attached to external hangers in the new "Victory Parade" design.

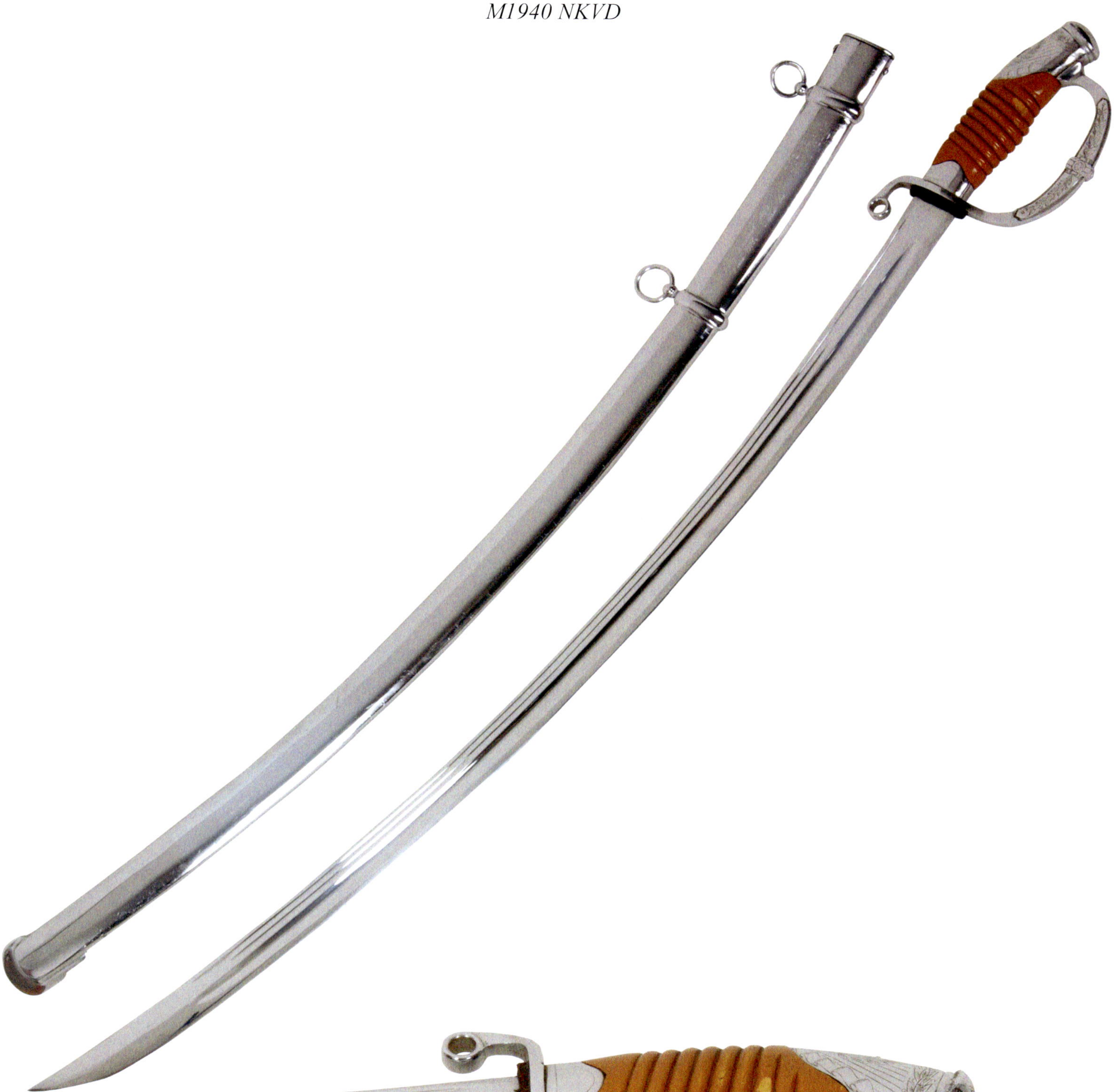

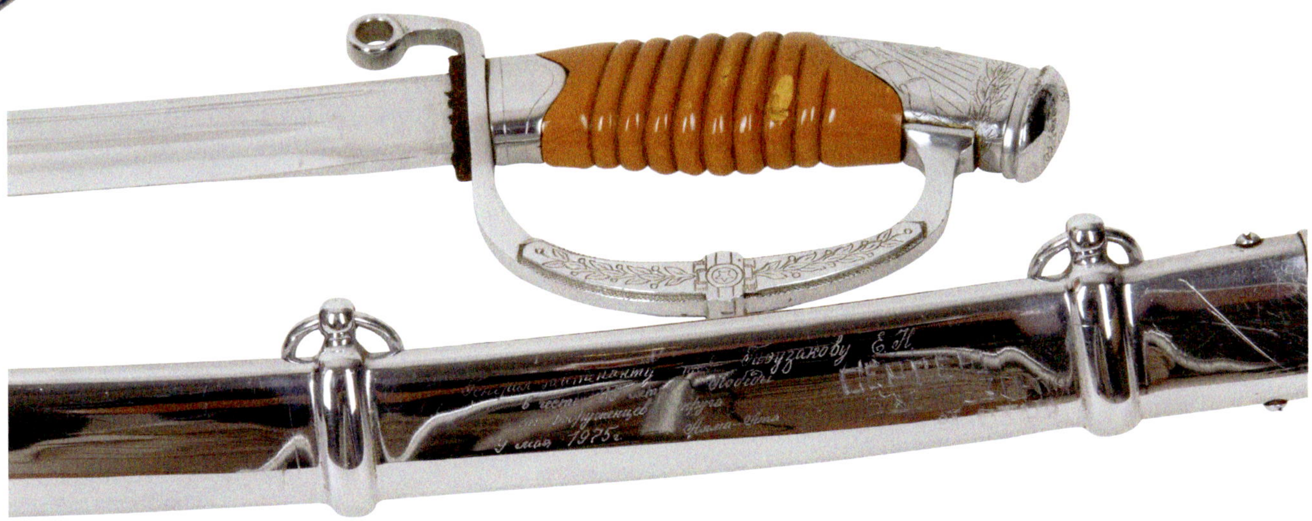

M1945

MARSHALS PARADE CROSS BELT

The M1943 silver parade belt was standard issue for marshals and generals after it replaced the M1940 leather belt in 1943 and 1944. The use of this silver, very Tsarist-looking belt did not last long, and plans were quickly under way for a new heavy gold brocade belt to replace it. This M1945 parade belt was not available for the June 1945 "Victory Parade," but was available for the victory celebrations after the surrender of the Japanese Empire later in the year. Unlike the M1943/44 silver parade belts that had a separate sword or dagger hanger belt worn under the tunic, the new M1945 belt had the hangers attached directly to the belt. An added, but rarely seen feature shown here, is a cross strap supporting the weight of the M1940 parade dress saber. In addition, the buckle has higher grade gold plating not found on standard issue belts. This extremely rare example is one of only very few known to exist.

A photograph of Colonel General Kuzma Petrovich Trubnikov. This photo was taken in the latter part of 1945, when Trubnikov was Assistant Commander in Chief Northern Group of Forces. He is wearing the M1945 parade belt that was issued in time for the "Victory over Japan" parades.

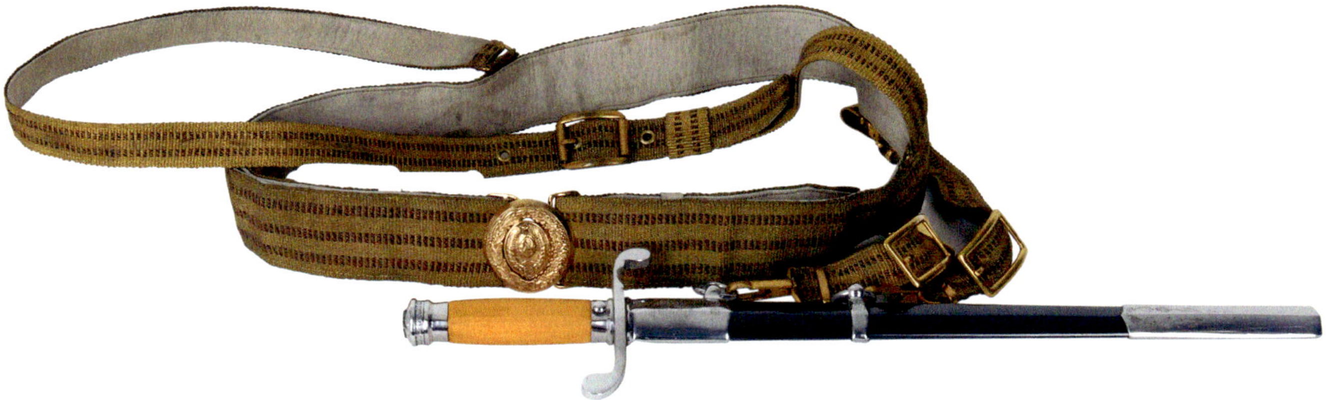

Prime Minister Winston Churchill, President Truman, and Marshal Stalin at the Potsdam Conference, July 17 to August 2, 1945.

Bibliography

Drabik, Douglas. "The Soviet M1945 Victory Parade Generals Dress Uniform." *The Military Advisor* 7.2 (Spring 1996): 4-9. Print

"The M1943 Uniform of the Soviet General." *The Military Advisor* 8.2 (Spring 1997): 30-35. Print.

"The Soviet M1945 Victory Parade Uniform of the Soviet Admiral and Naval General." *The Military Advisor* 9.2. (Spring 1998): 9-14. Print

"The M1940 Soviet Generals Uniform." *The Military Advisor* 11.3 (Summer 2000): 19-23. Print.

Drozdov, Georgi. *Victory Parade*. Moscow: Planeta, 1985. Print

Kutsenko, Anatoli. *Marshals and Fleet Admirals of the Soviet Union*. Kiev, Russia: Aspect Publishers, 2001. Print.

Lipatov, Pavel. *Uniforms of the Red Army*. Moscow: Teknika-Molodyozi, 2001. Print

McDaniel, Paul and Paul Schmitt. *The Comprehensive Guide to Soviet Orders and Medals*. Arlington, Virginia: Historical Research, 1997. Print.

Rutkiewicz, J. Wojska. *NKWD 1917-1946*. Warsaw: Barwa I Bron, 1998. Print.

Shalito, Anton. *Red Army Uniforms 1918-1945*. Moscow: Teknika-Molodyozi, 1999. Print.

Shishkov, Sergei. and Muzalevsky, Mikhail. *Orders and Medals of the USSR*. Vladivostok, Russia: Voron Publishers, 2001. Print

Shukman, Harold. *Stalin's Generals*. New York: Grove Press, 1993. Print.

Sinclair, James C. McComb and Douglas A. Drabik. *World War II Parade Uniforms of the Soviet Union: Marshals, Generals and Admirals*. Atglen, PA: Schiffer Military History, 2005. Print.

Suslov, Sergei. *Soviet Military Uniform and Insignia 1918-1958*.
Helsinki, Finland: Alga Fund Publishing, 1993. Print

Tokar, Leonid. *History of Russian Uniform: Soviet Police 1918-1991*. St.Petersburg, Russia: Exclusive Publishing House, 1995. Print